Taylor

B. Williams

Mozart's Story

Robina Beckles Willson

Illustrated by
Anthony Lewis

A & C Black · London

Music for Listening

A short list to enjoy.

Eine Kleine Nachtmusik (K525)

Piano Sonata in A (K331)

The Magic Flute (K620) Find the duet by Papageno and Papagena and the Birdcatcher's Song.

Clarinet Concerto (K622)

Sinfonia Concertante for violin and viola (K364)

Adagio and Rondo in C Minor for glass harmonica, flute, oboe, viola and cello (K617)

Piano Concerto No. 24 in C Minor (K491) (played at the benefit concert by Beethoven in 1795)

A Musical Joke (K522)

Horn Concerto No. 2 (K417)

Symphony No. 40 in G Minor (K550)

For Tony, with love and thanks

Grateful thanks are due to Rachel Beckles Willson, Catherine Burchill, Nicky Coldstream, Ilse Halbmayer (Vienna), Dr Peter Payan, John Shirley-Quirk, Dr Johanna Senigl (The Mozarteum, Salzburg), Dr Marian Zwiercan (Biblioteka Jagiellonska, Krakow)

The publishers gratefully acknowledge permission to reproduce photographs from the following: the Mozarteum, Salzburg pp 4, 5, 12, 13, 37, 42, 43, 47, The Royal Collection, pp 18, 40, the MozartSchifftung p 39, the British Museum pp 15, 22 the Horniman Museum p 21, the Louvre p 25

First published 1991 by A & C Black (Publishers) Ltd
35 Bedford Row, London, WC1R 4JH

Text copyright © 1991 Robina Beckles Willson
Illustrations © 1991 Anthony Lewis

ISBN 0 7136 3311 5

A CIP catalogue record for this book
is available from the British Library

Designed by Robert Wheeler Associates

Filmset by August Filmsetting, Haydock, St Helens
Printed and bound in Italy by L.E.G.O. Spa.

Contents

An Extraordinary Boy

Mozart must have heard music every day as a baby, because his father played the violin. His parents, Leopold and Anna Maria had seven children, but only two survived. One was Maria Anna Walpurga Ignatia, who was nicknamed Nannerl. She was four and a half years older than her brother who was born on January 27th 1756. He was christened Joannes Chrysostomus Wolfgang Gottlieb, but his family called him Wolfgang Amadeus.

They lived in Salzburg, in Austria, where Leopold was court composer to the Prince Archbishop. Leopold wrote church music and many pieces for special occasions. In the year that Mozart was born, his father's book, *Violin School* was published, giving advice on how to play the violin.

Although Leopold was very busy, he made time to teach his children. Nannerl had lessons on the harpsichord, and may have done her practice on the smaller clavichord. Wolfgang listened to Nannerl's music lessons and when he was three he began to reach up to the keyboard. He didn't just plink and plonk the keys, but tried out which notes sounded good together. He could even copy the tunes his sister played.

By the time Wolfang was four, he had persuaded his father to give him lessons too. Leopold was astonished at how quickly Wolfgang learned his pieces, and noted in Nannerl's music book:

This piece 'was learnt by Wolfgang within half an hour on 26th January 1761, a day before his fifth birthday, at about half past nine at night.'

Leopold Mozart wrote a famous book, Violin School

Wolfgang watched Leopold writing out his compositions and played pieces copied out for pupil's lessons. The young boy began to make up his own music, so Leopold began to copy down what Wolfgang composed.

He composed this minuet when he was six.

One day Leopold and Schachtner, the court trumpeter, found Wolfgang busy writing. The boy wasn't used to a dip pen and ink, and he'd made a lot of blots, wiped into smudges. The men thought he was only pretending to write music. But when they looked closely, they could make out notes. Leopold said they were too hard to play, but Wolfgang calmly explained that it was a concerto, which needed practice, and showed them what he was trying to compose on the harpsichord.

Wolfgang was born in a flat on the third floor of this house.

Wolfgang wasn't delighted by all musical sounds: the sound of Schachtner's trumpet terrified the boy until he was nearly nine. Leopold's plan to cure him of the fear didn't work: when the trumpet was deliberately blared at him, he almost fainted. But Wolfgang enjoyed the sweet sound of Schachtner's violin and nicknamed it a 'butter fiddle'. He was normally a cheerful boy, who was confident about his musical talent. One thing which did upset him was when his family teased him, and said they didn't love him any more.

Nannerl and Wolfgang both had daily lessons with their father. Leopold had begun to realise that while Nannerl was a good musician, Wolfgang might be a genius and he decided to give up his other pupils to concentrate on his son and daughter. He taught them German, Latin and Arithmetic. Wolfgang loved sums. Sometimes he was so carried away that he would work them out over the table and walls.

But the boy's life wasn't all hard work, and he played games as well as duets with his sister. Unlike many children when they learn to play an instrument, Wolfgang was sorry to stop practising. He included music in his games, too. He would sing and march in time to the music when he was putting his toys away, and invite any visiting musicians to join in.

Wolfgang had his own miniature violin and even before he'd had any proper lessons, he wanted to join in when his father played. He pleaded to be allowed to play one day when Leopold was trying out a new string trio with Schachtner and a pupil. Leopold said it was impossible, and Wolfgang cried. Schachtner kindly offered to let the boy play second violin alongside him. Leopold warned him to play quietly or he'd be sent away. But it was Schachtner who played quietly when he heard what Wolfgang could do. In the end he stopped playing and let the boy finish the piece. When Wolfgang tried out the first violin part, they all laughed at the way he had to jiggle his fingers to manage the music, but Schachtner noticed that 'they never stuck fast.'

At night, Wolfgang had invented a special ceremony for saying goodnight to his father. Every evening, at bedtime, he would stand on a chair and sing a nonsense song he'd made up:

> Oragno fiagata fa
> marina gamina fa

Leopold would join in to make a duet. Then Wolfgang would kiss him and go off happily. He promised that when his father was old, he would keep him in a glass case for safety.

Leopold was beginning to think that Salzburg was too small a place for his talented children. He believed their talents were given by God, and that it was his duty to show them to the world. He knew that they could also earn money as child performers: Nannerl was very clever and Wolfgang certainly was an extraordinary boy.

The First Journeys

IN JANUARY 1762, when Wolfgang was six, Leopold took the children to Munich to begin their performing careers. Musicians at that time earned their living from jobs given by the nobility. These supporters were called patrons. Sometimes the musicians were full time members of staff; sometimes they were paid for concerts or compositions. Composers might also earn money from having their music printed and sold. But if it was played in another town, they received no money.

The Mozarts stayed in lodgings, waiting to be summoned to play in front of noble households. Leopold would often have to wait days before he was paid.

Their playing as a trio was much admired, but audiences specially liked testing young Wolfgang. Someone would give him a tune and he would write a bass part for it, then add a violin part. He could accompany other players with great skill. And he played as a soloist in a keyboard concerto with an orchestra.

In September, the whole family set off for Vienna, the capital city of Austria. Today it takes about four hours by coach from Salzburg: the Mozart family took almost four weeks, covering only about fifty kilometres a day and stopping at an inn each evening. They travelled slowly and allowed time for the children to rest for a few days every now and then. Part of the journey was by boat from Linz on the river Danube. They paused at a monastery where Leopold wrote home to their landlord, 'our Woferl strummed on the organ.' He played so well that the monks and their guests rushed to see him and, Leopold said, 'were almost struck dead with amazement.'

Sometimes the family were invited to give concerts where they stayed, or in nearby stately homes. The nobles who heard them sent enthusiastic messages to their friends, and by the time the Mozarts reached Vienna, they were already well known. While they were stopped at customs, Wolfgang showed the officers his clavichord. Then he took out his violin and played to them. The officers were so fascinated that they charged no duties at all.

In Vienna, the family stayed in lodgings of one long narrow room with two beds and a partition. Leopold shared a bed with Wolfgang. He didn't think it was funny when his sleeping son dug him in the ribs and kicked him out of bed – and the same thing happened to Anna Maria with Nannerl. But they were prepared to put up with a lot just to be in Vienna.

Soon invitations began to arrive from Viennese lords and ladies, and Wolfgang performed twice most days. Each morning, the children would practise. On one hectic day, they were taken by carriage to play at half past two, then stayed till a quarter to four. Then a Count called for them and galloped them to play at a lady's house until half past five. Next, another Count sent his carriage for them and they stayed at his house until about nine o'clock.

The most exciting invitation came from the Emperor Franz 1. An imperial carriage was sent to take the whole family to his summer palace, Schönbrunn. After hearing him, the Emperor called Wolfgang a little wizard, and made him show off by playing with the keyboard covered. Wolfgang was more interested in playing a concerto by the court composer.

Nannerl, aged ten, wearing the gala costume given to her by the Empress of Austria.

Wolgang, aged six, wearing his gala costume. Both costumes were miniature versions of adult clothes.

Wolfgang was not frightened or shy when he played in front of the Emperor, and he wasn't over-awed by the imperial family either. He enjoyed playing with the children, especially Princess Marie Antoinette who was about the same age. Once he skidded and fell on the polished floor. She helped him up and Wolfgang turned around and asked her to marry him.

Wolfgang kissed the Empress. She was enchanted by him, and sent him and Nannerl gala costumes, which were miniature grown-up clothes first made for her children. Wolfgang's was a lilac jacket and breeches with matching silk waistcoat, trimmed with gold braid. Nannerl's dress was in white taffeta. Both wore white powdered wigs as if they were adults. The children gave many concerts, earned a lot of money, and had many late nights.

Wolfgang seemed to enjoy all the presents and fuss, and perhaps Nannerl did too. Leopold listed some of the presents they'd been given: swords, cloaks, coats, hats, Dutch lace, ladies' toilet bottles, needle cases, decorated snuff boxes, gold watches, gold shoe-buckles, a gold tooth-pick case, a silver pocket writing-case with silver pens, rings, ribbons, and other things. He would have preferred to receive money, because travelling and lodgings were expensive.

Suddenly, at the end of October, Wolfgang became ill. He developed painful spots and a high temperature. As medicine, Leopold gave him a black powder, and then another powder. A doctor was called, who said that it was a sort of scarlet fever. Leopold and Anna Maria were very worried: scarlet fever was then a dangerous disease which killed thousands of children every year. They took great care to nurse Wolfgang back to health and he gradually began to recover from the fever. Then he started to cut a back tooth, which made his cheek swell up. When Leopold cancelled Wolfgang's engagements, the nobles heard about his illness and sent messages asking after him. It was four weeks before the rash had disappeared and Wolfgang was well enough to give concerts and earn again. Leopold was simply relieved that Wolfgang had recovered.

Altogether, the family was away in Vienna for four months. The children's performances improved steadily. Wolfgang could sight-read any music put in front of him, and could improvise, making up music as he played. He most enjoyed meeting musicians and hearing new music all the time.

When the family returned home to Salzburg, Leopold was given a better job, in spite of all the time he had spent away. But his main ambitions were for his children: he arranged for his son's early pieces to be published, and began to plan an international tour. Wolfgang was already being called a Wunderkind, or Wonderchild, and Leopold longed to show him off as an amazing musician. He set his sights on Paris as a fashionable place to visit.

Wolfgang loved travelling in fast carriages and being on the move. In a letter, his father said, 'Wolfgang is extraordinarily jolly, but a bit of a scamp as well.' Crossing Germany, he invented his own imaginary country, where he was King and Nannerl was his subject. He called the kingdom 'Rücken' or 'Back', and persuaded their servant to draw a map of it while he dictated the names of cities, towns and villages. Sometimes the travel could be slow and boring: once they were held up for over half a day by a broken back wheel. Perhaps Wolfgang retreated to his country when wheels broke or coaches tipped over, or the muddy tracks slowed them down.

The family set off again for Munich on June 9th 1763. The family performed for the Elector, ruler of Bavaria, who was an old friend. Then they travelled slowly on to Augsburg, the town where Leopold had grown up. The children gave three concerts there. Leopold must have been specially proud when he wrote home that Nannerl's playing was much admired. He bought the children a portable clavier for their practice. He worked the children very hard, but they didn't complain. Occasionally Wolfgang was homesick because he missed his musician friends at home.

This portrait was used by Leopold for publicity ▷

The family were welcomed at Mannheim, their next stop. The orchestra gave the Mozarts a special concert which lasted for four hours. Next they travelled to Frankfurt and across to Brussels where they spent a few weeks.

On November 18th, the Mozarts arrived at Paris. They stayed with friends, who lent them a harpsichord for practising. The children gave several concerts. Leopold wrote home that 'my children have taken almost everyone by storm' but he didn't really like France. He thought that the women wore too much detestable make-up.

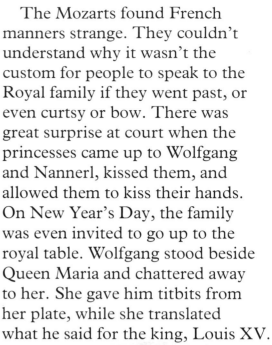

The Mozarts found French manners strange. They couldn't understand why it wasn't the custom for people to speak to the Royal family if they went past, or even curtsy or bow. There was great surprise at court when the princesses came up to Wolfgang and Nannerl, kissed them, and allowed them to kiss their hands. On New Year's Day, the family was even invited to go up to the royal table. Wolfgang stood beside Queen Maria and chattered away to her. She gave him titbits from her plate, while she translated what he said for the king, Louis XV.

The Mozart family had a busy time in Paris: Leopold took Wolfgang to hear the services in the Royal chapel at the Palace of Versailles; the children were introduced to French composers who gave them copies of their music, even though they were envious of the children's talents. With great pride, Leopold arranged for the printing of four of Wolfgang's sonatas for clavier and violin and wrote, '. . . every day God performs fresh miracles through this child.'

The family spent a lot of this visit waiting to be seen by patrons, getting permission to hold concerts or making arrangements for ticket selling. Leopold was worried in case the family was spending more money than they earned from concerts. He was grateful when a friend helped them by paying for sixty large and expensive wax candles, needed for their first concert. But the Mozart family weren't always short of money: while they were in Paris, Leopold could afford to have a picture painted of himself playing with his children.

Although the family were successful in France, Leopold was ready to move on. He arranged for prayers to be said at home for their safe crossing of the Channel to England.

A Long Visit to London

T HE MOZARTS WERE all very sick crossing the Channel, although Leopold was quite sure that he was the most ill. They spent their first night in London at a coach-inn in Piccadilly, then moved to lodgings in the house of Mr Cousin, a hairdresser who lived near Charing Cross.

Only a few days later, on April 27th 1764, they were invited to play for King George III and Queen Charlotte at court. The children played by themselves and with other musicians. Leopold found their welcome warmer than at any other court, and wrote, 'their easy manner and friendly ways made us forget that they were King and Queen of England.'

A week later the family were walking in St James Park when the king drove by. He opened his carriage window and greeted them, especially Wolfgang. Leopold was impressed to be recognised at all. He thought that English clothes looked like fancy dress. His wife and daughter were already decked out in new hats and Wolfgang had a new outfit.

During his visit to London, Wolfgang played for King George III and the royal family.

The children were asked to take part in many concerts and in May they were invited to court again. This time they stayed from six until ten in the evening for a small royal family gathering. Wolfgang played the harpsichord and the organ and sight-read music by Bach, Handel and other composers. He accompanied the Queen when she sang, then did some improvisation at the keyboard. Everyone was amazed by his talent.

Encouraged by this royal interest, Leopold set about winning the support of the aristocracy. In his travel diary, he made long lists of the noblemen and ambassadors on whom he paid calls with his children.

In many other places the family had only played to private audiences, but London was already famous for public concerts so Leopold decided to arrange one for June 5th 1764. It was a risk to hold it in summer as many families were away in the country, but Leopold had worked out that some people would be back in London for the King's birthday on June 4th.

Leopold put an advertisement in the *Public Advertiser*:

'For the Benefit of Miss Mozart of Eleven, and Master Mozart of Seven Years of Age, Prodigies of Na(ture). This Method is therefore taken to show to the Public the greatest Prodigy that Europe or that even Human Nature has to boast of. Every Body will be struck with Admiration to hear them, and particularly to hear a young Boy of seven Years of Age play on the Harpsichord with such Dexterity and Perfection. It surpasses all Understanding or all Imagination; and it is hard to say whether his Execution upon the Harpsichord, and his playing at Sight, or his own Compositions, are most astonishing.'

Leopold cheated a little in trying to attract an audience as Wolfgang was already over eight.

They only had a few days to sell tickets so Leopold was thrilled when over two hundred people bought them, 'including,' as Leopold wrote, 'the leading people in all London.'

The concert was held in the Great Room in Spring Garden, not far from their lodgings. Although the Mozarts had to pay rent for hall, pay for the lighting, hire the music stands and two harpsichords, they made a profit of ninety guineas. Best of all, the children were successfully launched as performers.

As another way of being noticed and of winning support, Leopold allowed Wolfgang to play the organ at a charity concert to raise money for a maternity hospital. It was held at the Rotunda in Ranelagh Gardens, a well known concert hall. People crowded to hear the young performer.

Leopold thought it would be good for the children to meet other musicians and instrument makers. A famous opera singer, Manzuoli, was so impressed by Wolfgang's musical gifts that he offered to teach the boy singing. Wolfgang liked the Queen's music master, Johann Christian Bach, the son of the composer Johann Sebastian Bach. Bach, like other musicians, treated the boy as an equal although there was twenty one years difference in age. Wolfgang learned a lot from him. Once, when Bach was playing the organ, he sat Wolfgang between his knees so that they could take it in turns to improvise. They continued for two hours, and people listening couldn't tell which one of them was playing.

The family may have gone to see one of Bach's operas, which was first shown in London in 1765. Wolfgang fell in love with opera. He started to make up an opera in his head and began to make a list of the players he would like in his orchestra.

While they were in London, the family went to visit Benjamin Franklin who, as well as being a scientist and American statesman, was a talented musician. He had noticed a craze for playing drinking glasses by rubbing their rims and from this had invented an instrument called the Harmonica. This was a set of glass bowls of graded sizes fixed to a revolving rod turned by a pedal. The player stroked the glasses with a damp finger to give a sweet piercing tone. Wolfgang was intrigued and later composed music for the instrument.

Wolfgang composed for the Harmonica, an instrument made of revolving glass bowls.

Not all the children's time was spent visiting, practising and performing. Nannerl kept a diary where she described the sightseeing they did. She mentioned seeing an elephant and a zebra in a park, visiting the Tower of London, Westminster Bridge, and driving out to see the view from Richmond Hill and the Royal Gardens at Kew.

The house in Chelsea where the Mozart family stayed.

But all this hectic activity suddenly came to a halt. One summer evening, Leopold couldn't get a carriage to take them across London. Instead he hired a sedan chair for the children, and decided to walk behind. But the journey would take half an hour, and Leopold had forgotten how fast the London bearers jogged. He got very hot and then chilled so much that he had to hire another sedan to carry him. All this gave him a cold and a raging sore throat. He said he felt so ill he thought he was going to die.

'In England,' he wrote, 'there is a kind of native complaint, which is called a "cold". That is why you hardly ever see people wearing summer clothes... The wisest course... is to leave England and cross the sea.'

But all he could do was move the family out of town for his convalescence. They went to Chelsea, which was then a village surrounded by fields.

At the beginning of their stay, they had meals sent in from an eating house, a kind of eighteenth century take-away. But the family didn't like the cooking so Anna Maria took over while her husband rested.

The children had a rest from practising their instruments, as Leopold couldn't even bear the sound of music. Wolfgang used the time to compose piano pieces. The sketch book he used shows how he worked by himself on a collection of 43 pieces, which became more original and complicated as he went on. Most are piano pieces. A few seem to be sketches of works for more instruments, written down as piano arrangements. He began to write a symphony for 'all the instruments of the orchestra, but especially for trumpets and kettledrums'. Nannerl sat beside him copying it out. Wolfgang asked her to remind him 'to give the horns something worthwhile to do.'.

The family stayed quietly in Chelsea for about seven weeks until Leopold felt strong enough to start 'galloping round' again, organising exhibition performances. From their lodgings, he sold prints of the family portrait and copies of Wolfgang's sonatas. He posted some of these home to be sold at half price because he wanted ' to encourage young people in Salzburg to study music with zest.'

Wolfgang dedicated a new set of harpsichord sonatas to the Queen, who played this instrument. Leopold was approached by the trustees of the British Museum who asked him to donate some of Wolfgang's compositions. The Mozarts gave them a copy of the family picture and some sonatas, the first music ever presented to the British Museum. The most interesting item was the manuscript of a four part piece for voices, *God is our Refuge!*, which can still be seen there.

The British Museum had only been open a few years when Wolfgang gave them his manuscript of God is our Refuge! *Wolfgang copied out his music and Leopold helped to write out some of the words.*

Wolfgang's fame as a performer was spreading. Daines Barrington, a scientist and keen musician, heard the boy play and decided to visit the family to test Wolfgang's skills. He asked Wolfgang to sight-read music and to sing a high part while Leopold sang the low one. Then he asked the boy to make up a typical operatic Love Song, then a Song of Rage. Wolfgang threw himself into his music, so that Barrington said 'in the middle of it, he had worked himself up to such a pitch that he beat his harpsichord like a person possessed,'.

Barrington was so impressed that he thought Leopold
was lying about Wolfgang's age, and was only convinced
when he saw the boy fooling about: 'Whilst he was
playing to me, a favourite cat came in, upon which he
immediately left his harpsichord, nor could we bring him
back for a considerable time.' Barrington was even more
amused to see Wolfgang riding his hobby-horse.

The Mozart family stayed in London for nearly 15
months. Leopold hinted in his letters that he had been
asked to stay in England, but he didn't approve of the way
children were brought up. He decided to move on.

His last notice in the *Public Advertiser* offered
performances 'every Day in the Week, from Twelve to
Three o'Clock in the Great Room, at the Swan and Hoop,
Cornhill. Admittance 2s 6d each Person.

'The two Children will play also with four hands upon
the same harpsichord and put upon it a Handkerchief
without seeing the Keys.'

Soon it was time to leave, and there was a great deal to
arrange. Leopold said that just the sight of all the luggage
they had to pack made him perspire. But he was pleased
with their stay and all that Wolfgang had learnt: he
boasted that his young son knew 'what one would expect
from a man of forty.'

The First View of Italy

THE MOZARTS LEFT London on July 24th 1765, and stayed near Canterbury till the end of the month to see some horse racing. Leopold had decided to visit Holland next, to visit the Prince of Orange, but the family were held up in France with bad colds for four weeks. They finally arrived at the Hague and met the Prince and his sister, but very soon afterwards, Nannerl fell ill with typhoid.

She had such a high temperature that she became delirious and talked in her sleep in German, English and French. It sounded so funny that it cheered up her brother a little. But Leopold was afraid she was going to die and sent for a priest to pray for her. He and Anna Maria shared the nursing because they didn't want a stranger to look after their child, taking it in turns to get up after only five hours sleep. Nannerl gradually recovered, but just as she felt better, Wolfgang caught the fever and became so weak that he even had to be carried from his bed to a chair.

Leopold's usual careful arrangements were upset. He had already sent on a trunk full of fur coats and rugs to Paris ready for the winter, yet the family were still in Holland in December. It was several weeks before the children were well enough to give concerts at the Hague and Amsterdam.

They travelled on to Paris where they stayed for two months. The newspapers were full of stories about the famous children. By the autumn, the family had moved on to Switzerland, and then to Munich, where they were again delayed when Wolfgang had rheumatic fever so badly that he couldn't stand. Finally, at the end of

November 1765, they returned home to Salzburg after more than three years away.

The long tour had been a success, but had also been expensive. Leopold started to raise money by selling off unwanted presents. He'd also brought back things from abroad which were rare in Salzburg so that he could sell them at a profit.

Wolfgang was now very famous in his home town. Leopold told people that only those who saw and heard him would believe his progress. The Prince Archbishop Schrattenbach wanted to find out for himself. With Leopold's permission he locked Wolfgang on his own with just some sheets of paper and a pen, to test if the boy really could compose without any help from his father. He was so impressed by the music Wolfgang composed that he asked the boy to write his first operatic piece, called *Apollo and Hyacinthus*.

Gossips in Salzburg couldn't believe that the Mozart family would be happy to stay at home after their successful tour. Some people thought they might visit Scandinavia and Russia, perhaps even China. Certainly Leopold wasn't satisfied to stay in Salzburg when he heard that in Vienna, the Archduchess Maria Josepha was going to be married. In September 1767, Leopold took the children to Vienna.

Wolfgang playing the harpsichord for the Prince de Conti and his friends in Paris.

25

Things didn't go as expected. There was a terrible outbreak of smallpox, which at that time was very common, and rather like a dangerous kind of chickenpox. The bride died from it, so the wedding was cancelled. The Mozart family left Vienna, to try to avoid the disease, but it was too late. Both Nannerl and Wolfgang had already caught it.

A kind friend offered to take the family into his home, so they carried Wolfgang from the inn, packed up in leather wrappings and furs. Leopold had great faith in his medicinal black powders but he was still very anxious to see Wolfgang's red hot cheeks and ice cold hands. Nannerl, whose smallpox was less severe, noticed that her brother's eyes were so sore that for days he could hardly see.

At last the children began to recover. When Wolfgang felt better, he became bored staying in bed, and passed the time learning card tricks.

The family weren't able to return to Vienna until January 1768, but when they did, they were welcomed warmly at court. The Emperor Joseph II invited Wolfgang to write a comic opera in Italian for the imperial theatre and to conduct it himself. Wolfgang agreed and by July, he had finished *La Finta Semplice* or *The Pretend Simpleton*. But other composers at court were jealous of Wolfgang. They spread rumours that his father had composed the opera, that singers could not sing their music and that the orchestra did not like being conducted by a twelve year old boy. In spite of Leopold's angry protests, the opera was not performed until the following year, in Salzburg.

The Mozarts spent nearly a year at home. Leopold's employer, the Archbishop Schrattenbach, gave Wolfgang a job with the title, Concert Master to the Court Music. Leopold asked for leave to visit Italy and study opera. Schrattenbach realised that Leopold was ambitious for the boy and gave his permission. Father and son and a servant set off, carrying with them many letters recommending them to possible patrons.

In 1770, Wolfgang started to write home for the first time. Because paper was so expensive, he used to write in the gaps between the lines in his father's letters. He wrote as if he was speaking: teasing his sister, sending funny and sometimes rude jokes, or grumbles, writing in four different languages in turn and sending millions of kisses. But music was always the main subject of his letters.

His first letter home, when he was 14, began:

Dearest mamma!
My heart is completely enchanted . . . because it is so jolly on this journey, because it is so warm in the carriage and because our coachman is a fine fellow who, when the road gives him the slightest chance, drives so fast.

Leopold was less happy about the journey:

I cannot write to anybody for I am hustled to death. Nothing but packing and unpacking, and withal no warm room so that one freezes like a dog.

In spite of the wintry roads, they travelled rapidly across Italy, seeing operas at Mantua, Verona and Milan. Wolfgang sent descriptions home of Italian singers and ballets: he thought the minuet was danced very slowly in Italy. He sent home some country dances and asked the court dancing master to make up some steps for them. Leopold and Wolfgang were both very busy, composing and copying out the parts. In Milan, Wolfgang was asked to write an opera for Christmas. He was very popular and played to huge audiences.

Father and son moved on to Bologna for three months. Wolfgang was taught by Padre Martini, a scholar and teacher who had earlier taught Johann Christian Bach. Wolfgang admired his teacher and they became close friends.

Usually, Wolfgang didn't have time to make friends of his own age but when he and his father moved to Florence, he met an English boy called Thomas Linley. The two boys liked each other immediately. Thomas was a brilliant violinist, also touring, and when they first met, they took it in turns to play all evening, each becoming more and more excited. Both were very upset when the Mozarts had to leave the next day, and they promised to stay friends. They wrote letters, but Wolfgang never saw Thomas again.

Leopold and Wolfgang continued their journey. In Naples there was a rumour that Wolfgang could only play brilliantly when he was wearing a magic ring. So when he took off the ring and played just as superbly, the audience was very impressed. Wolfgang and his father spent a few days sight-seeing round the area, looking at ancient temples and Roman ruins. Wolfgang enjoyed watching Vesuvius 'smoking furiously'.

Thomas Linley was exactly the same age as Wolfgang. They met in Florence where Thomas was also performing.

In Rome, when the Mozarts went to see the Pope, people
mistakenly thought Wolfgang was a Prince, with Leopold his tutor.
Father and son visited St Peter's Church to kiss the feet of the statue
of St Peter. Wolfgang was so small that he had to be lifted up so he
could reach. Later he went to the Sistine Chapel, where he heard a
beautiful piece meant only to be sung by the Pope's choir. Leopold
wrote to his wife that Wolfgang was able to remember every note of
this piece and write it out afterwards.

Wolfgang received his greatest honour from the Pope, who made
him a Knight of the Golden Spur. He was presented with a golden
cross on a red sash, a sword and some spurs, and was entitled to be
called Signor Cavaliere.

But Wolfgang was sometimes homesick. He wrote asking after the
canary and teasing Nannerl about a boyfriend. He missed the
Sunday afternoon contests when the family and their friends shot at
targets. In one letter he mockingly described, in Italian, a rather dull
day: he woke up at nine, or sometimes ten, then he went out with his
father. For lunch they would go to an eating-house, and after lunch
they wrote music or went out again. Then they had supper of half a
chicken or a small slice of roast meat.

After Rome, they went back to Bologna, and planned to travel on to Milan, stopping at Florence where Wolfgang hoped to see Thomas again. But this plan was ruined. One of the horses pulling the Mozart's carriage fell down and dragged it over. Leopold's leg was gashed so badly that he had to spend three weeks in bed and another seven resting. They were forced to stay in Bologna, which made Leopold worry about the cost of the delay.

When they were ready to leave, they were delayed again: Wolfgang was honoured by the Accademia Filarmonica. He had to take a musical test in a locked room, which he finished more quickly than almost anyone else who had done it. The usual rule was that a musician had to be more than twenty years old to receive this honour, but the rule was broken for Wolfgang.

In October, Leopold and Wolfgang travelled to Milan in bad weather. Wolfgang had finished his opera, *Mitridate*. By December, they were rehearsing it with an orchestra of sixty players. He had trouble with a jealous rival who tried to prevent the prima donna from singing his music by replacing it with another composer's. Otherwise rehearsals went smoothly and the first performance took place on December 26th. The work lasted for six hours including two hours of ballet, with Wolfgang conducting from the keyboard throughout. He was rewarded with many encores and cheers of 'Long live the little Master'.

After sixteen months travel in Italy, Leopold and Wolfgang returned home, but only for a few months. Then they went back to Milan so that Wolfgang could compose some music for a royal wedding. He wrote to his sister:

'Upstairs we have a violinist, downstairs another one, in the next room a singing-master who gives lessons, and in another room opposite ours an oboist. It is good fun when you are composing! It gives you plenty of ideas.'

At only fifteen Wolfgang was a famous performer and composer. He had written thirteen symphonies and his first string quartet as well as many shorter pieces. But the day after he returned home in triumph to Salzburg, his father's employer, the Archbishop, died, and Wolfgang's life was changed.

Travelling and Job Hunting

THE NEW PRINCE ARCHBISHOP was called Colloredo. He thought of his musicians as servants whose duty was to stay at court in Salzburg. He expected the sixteen year old Wolfgang to be grateful for his small salary and made it difficult for him to accept invitations from other places to perform or compose.

Leopold managed to arrange to take his son back to Italy in the autumn of 1772 to finish the opera *Lucio Silla* which Wolfgang was composing for the Christmas carnival in Milan. On the day of the first full rehearsal, Wolfgang wrote to Nannerl:

> 'Think of me, my dear sister, and try as hard as you can to imagine that you, my dear sister, are hearing and seeing it too.'

Wolgang's opera was a success, although there were some problems on the first night: a packed audience had to wait three hours until the Archduke and his wife arrived. The tenor singer had never performed on such a big stage before. He exaggerated his movements so that when he was supposed to look angry, he only made the audience laugh. This upset the prima donna who didn't sing well for the rest of the evening. Nevertheless the opera had twenty-five more performances.

During his stay, Wolfgang wrote six quartets. He liked composing for talented musicians, but this didn't give him a steady income. All his experience with singers and players did not produce a job, so he returned with his father to Salzburg in March 1773.

There was plenty for Wolfgang to do at home, but he was unhappy. He resented the Archbishop's domineering attitude to his musicians, so he was delighted to go to Vienna in July while the Archbishop was away. Wolfgang would have liked to have found a different job, but his father warned him that gossip about this from rival

musicians might reach Colloredo. And although in
Vienna, Wolfgang met the Empress and performed for
many people, there was no invitation to work.

Mozart was still as cheerful as ever. He wrote jokey letters to his
sister, calling her 'my heart, my lung, my stomach'. He asked about
their fox terrier:

'How is Miss Bimbes? Please give her all sorts of messages from
me.'

He finished with 'greetings to all my good friends'
and signed the letter 'Gnagflow Trazom'.

In the autumn of 1773, Wolfgang and his father went back to
Salzburg and the family moved to a larger home across the river.
They had eight first floor rooms to live in so there was more space.
Leopold used the biggest room to display and sell harpsichords and
clavichords.

Even though Wolfgang felt restless, he had many good friends at
home. One was the Archbishop's musical director, Michael Haydn.
Wolfgang liked Michael and studied his works, as well as the string
quartets of his friend's famous brother, Joseph Haydn.

Wolfgang was still pleased to get away again, this time
to prepare a comic opera, *La Finta Giardiniera*, (*The
Pretend Gardener*) for performance in Munich. Leopold

went ahead with his son in December 1774, and sent careful instructions for Nannerl, who was joining them for the first performance:

> 'Nannerl must certainly have a fur rug for the journey . . . she must wrap up her head well and she must protect her feet with something more than her felt shoes . . . She ought therefore to slip on the fur boots which she will find in the trunk under the roof.'

A foot bag surrounded by hay completed the list.

The first performance of *La Finta Giardiniera*, in front of the Elector of Bavaria and his court, was a great success. Wolfgang wrote to his mother about the packed first night when people had to be turned away, and of the tremendous applause and shouts of 'Bravo maestro.' He asked her not to hope for his early return to Salzburg as she would realise 'how much good it is doing me to be able to breathe freely.' In fact, Colloredo passed through Munich and heard all the praise of Mozart from the Elector and the courtiers. But he was too embarrassed to do anything except shrug.

On Wolfgang's return to Salzburg, Colloredo asked him to write a festival opera to celebrate the visit of the Emperor's brother, Archduke Maximilian. The opera *Il Re Pastore* (The Shepherd King) was performed in 1775. The young composer spent all the following year at home. He enjoyed writing harpsichord concertos and short pieces for groups of instruments such as wind bands, as well as symphonies and church music.

But Wolfgang had toured so much as a child that he became restless. He and his father applied to their employer several times for permission to travel. The Archbishop refused. Wolfgang asked to resign from being a 'part-time servant': the Archbishop said that Wolfgang and his father could both leave his service. Leopold was so horrified at the thought of being out of work that he felt ill. He humbly went to the Archbishop to ask for his own job back.

So, in 1777, the family was now split in two: Anna Maria was to travel with Wolfgang, while Nannerl and Leopold stayed in Salzburg. Leopold missed the sound of Wolfgang's practice. Nannerl became a keen housewife. Her father said that she was 'for ever poking her nose into the kitchen' and scolding the maid about dirt.

For the first time, Wolfgang wasn't going to have his father at his side to arrange everything so that the young man could simply make music or relax and rest. At twenty one, he had never even done his own packing. On the journey to Munich, he tried to take charge, and wrote home: 'I am quite a second Papa, for I see to everything . . . The porter knocked at the door and asked about all sorts of things, and I answered him with my most serious air, looking just as I do in my portrait.' But Wolfgang was still mischievous enough to send jokes home about Colloredo to whom he gave a rude nickname, Mufti HC. Leopold warned him that their letters might be opened by spies working for the Archbishop.

Wolfgang hoped that the Elector of Munich would be so impressed by his music that he would be offered a permanent job, but there was no vacancy. Wolfgang found it hard to understand: he knew he was talented. Leopold had told his son to make friends with anybody who was powerful, but courtly bowing and scraping did not come easily to Wolfgang. He wondered if he might even be better off somewhere else, where they appreciated musicians more.

He and his mother moved on to Augsburg, where they stayed with relations. He was still no good at packing. Anna Maria complained:

'. . . I am sweating so that the water is pouring down my face, simply from the fag of packing. The devil take all travelling. I feel that I could shove my feet into my mug, I am so exhausted.'

Wolfgang played brilliantly at Augsburg. He was using a new piano which didn't jangle like some other instruments. Some people listening thought Wolfgang was inspired by God. But this concert didn't make much money.

Their four month visit to Mannheim, a town well known for its excellent orchestra, didn't make much money either. As composers were beginning to write opera in German, Wolfgang expected to be given work. But he couldn't make a living from his music. At home Leopold ran up debts trying to support their tour and found this shameful. Wolfgang didn't help matters by sending wild, impractical money-making ideas to his worried father.

Wolfgang did do some teaching and composing, but he was easily led astray by his friends. His mother said he was 'too generous, not pushing and too easily taken in.' He was certainly a better judge of music than of people.

He made friends with the Weber family. The father was a singer and music copyist who had five daughters and one son. The second daughter was sixteen year old Aloysia. Wolfgang was very impressed by her singing and took her with her father to court in Holland to sing to the Princess. He coached her in singing and wrote her a song. Gradually he fell in love with her.

He wrote home that he had the brilliant idea of taking Aloysia to Italy, with her father and elder sister, to make her fortune in opera, even though Aloysia had never appeared on the stage before.

Leopold was horrified. He knew that Wolfgang couldn't possibly earn a living that way. He ordered his son 'Off with you to Paris and . . . soon! Find your place among great people'. It was very hard on Wolfgang, but he was used to doing what he was told. His mother had been looking forward to going home, but instead she stayed with him and they set off for Paris in March 1778.

It was not a happy visit. People were quite interested in Wolfgang when he first arrived, but the only work he could find was teaching, or the badly paid job of organist at Versailles, which he decided not to take. He was pining for Aloysia. He was scornful about the 'shrieking howling' French singers and he didn't compose very much.

The lodgings Anna Maria and Wolfgang took were so tiny there wasn't even room to get a harpsichord up the stairs, so Wolfgang had to work at a friend's house. His mother became very lonely. She worried about how much food and rent were costing. Miserable and a long way from home, she became ill. Wolfgang tried all the family remedies, and found a German doctor to treat her, but it was no use. Anna Maria died.

This portrait was painted about two years after Anna Maria died. Her picture looks down on her family.

Wolfgang wrote to a friend to ask them to break the wretched news gently to Leopold, whom he knew would be heartbroken. Then he wrote a letter telling his father what had happened. He gave up trying to please the French: they didn't like him so he didn't like them. But Wolfgang didn't want to go straight home. The Weber family had moved to Munich. He went to see them.

Wolfgang hoped that Aloysia would return his love, but she didn't. She even mocked him about his red mourning coat.

In Salzburg, Leopold was still trying to find a job for his son which would pull them out of debt. He finally persuaded the Archbishop to offer Wolfgang the chance to be Court Organist. Wolfgang didn't really want the job. He didn't want to give up his independence. But he hadn't found a job for himself and he wasn't earning enough by giving concerts. When Leopold wrote to him to come and 'Console me', his son could not refuse.

Wolfgang returned to Salzburg and worked hard for more than eighteen months, but he was relieved when the chance came to write another opera. 'Idomeneo' was written for performance in Munich, and Leopold and Nannerl travelled to see the opening night.

In March 1781, Wolfgang's employer, Colloredo, visited Vienna, taking all his courtiers and servants with him. Wolfgang would have enjoyed this visit, except that the Archbishop would not allow him to perform for other people. And Wolfgang hated being made to eat and live with the servants.

One day the Archbishop ordered Wolfgang to deliver a parcel to Salzburg for him. It was an awkward task and Wolfgang said no. Colloredo lost his temper and called the young man a scoundrel. In a fury, Wolfgang resigned and rushed away.

He wrote a letter to say that he was leaving the Archbishop's service. But when he delivered this to the Chief Steward, they quarrelled and Wolfgang was kicked out.

Success and sadness in Vienna

WOLFGANG AMADEUS MOZART was still only twenty-five. He felt hurt and angry, but suddenly he was free from 'slavery in Salzburg'. He had many plans and hopes for the future which he described in long letters to his family. He even suggested that Nannerl could join him in Vienna to make her living.

Mozart began to arrange his own days, getting up at six, composing from seven till nine, and teaching till one. He would often go out for lunch, performing and meeting people. If he was not performing at a concert, he would work in the evening until nine when he would go out. He came home at about half past ten and composed sometimes until one o'clock in the morning.

The Weber family had also moved to Vienna. Aloysia was now married, to an actor called Joseph Lange. Mozart lodged with the family for a while, but people started to gossip about him and Constanze, Aloysia's younger sister, so he moved out, but only round the corner.

Constanze Weber was the younger sister of Mozart's first love, Aloysia.

By the end of 1781 Mozart admitted that he had fallen in love with Constanze. Leopold and Nannerl were afraid that he was being pushed into marriage by Constanze's mother. Mrs Weber tried to make Mozart sign a document promising to marry her daughter or pay 300 guilders a year. Constanze tore it up.

Mozart introduced Constanze to Franz Joseph Haydn, a new friend and a composer whom he greatly admired. They tried out string quartets with other friends, Mozart playing the viola part. He asked for advice and played new compositions, including pieces from his operas, to 'Papa' Haydn.

During his time in Vienna, Mozart composed seventeen piano concertos. He often took the solo part himself and improvised extra flourishes which delighted the audience.

Mozart's 'one joy and passion' was to compose. Constanze's younger sister described how she seemed to have his music on his brain all the time:

Mozart and Haydn were close friends. Mozart called him 'Papa' Haydn.

'Even when he was washing his hands when he rose in the morning, he walked up and down in the room the while, never standing still, tapped one heel against the other the while and always deep in thought . . . Also his hands and fet were always in motion, he was always playing with something e.g. his hat, pockets, watch-fob, tables, chairs, as if they were a clavier.'

In 1782, Mozart took part in a musical contest against an Italian pianist, arranged by Emperor Joseph II. Mozart hoped the Emperor would be so impressed that he would be offered a job, but nothing happened. However he was collecting sponsors for his concerts and beginning to do well.

Leopold was pleased at his son's success, but still not happy about Constanze. In July, Mozart asked his father's permission to marry her. In August, he went ahead with the wedding, even before his father's consent had arrived. Mozart was twenty six and his bride was twenty.

Mozart began to compose a Mass to celebrate their marriage. He taught Constanze the piano, and she also sang well. They meant to visit Leopold in Salzburg as soon as possible, but were held up by Constanze becoming pregnant and Mozart's attempts to find work. Leopold accused his son of putting things off. He and

Mozart's piano

Nannerl still didn't think Constanze was good enough to be the wife of their Wolfgang, although Constanze tried to be friendly.

They only managed to visit Salzburg after their baby was born. Sadly, he died in the care of a nurse while they were away.

In Salzburg, the young Mozarts visited all their old friends, including Michael Haydn, who was working for the Archbishop. Michael fell ill and couldn't finish six violin duets he had promised his employer, so Mozart wrote the last two duets for his friend, very fast and using his skill at imitating another composer's style of music.

Mozart's Mass in C minor, written for Constanze, was first performed in Salzburg on 26th October. The next morning, he and Constanze left Salzburg.

The following year Mozart's compositions and performances became more and more popular: everyone was talking about him. Constanze had a second baby, Karl Thomas. Nannerl had married a widower with five children and they lived just outside Salzburg so Mozart thought that his father might be lonely and invited him to Vienna. Leopold arrived in February 1785. He found his son's life hectic, and wrote to Nannerl in his weekly letter:

'Every day there are concerts; and the whole time is given up to teaching, music, composing and so forth. I feel rather out of it all. If only the concerts were over. It is impossible for me to describe the rush and bustle. Since my arrival, your brother's fortepiano has been taken to the theatre or to some other house at least 12 times since I have been here.'

Mozart had a pet starling which could almost sing a tune from one of his piano concertos.

Although Leopold grumbled, he was pleased about Mozart's subscription concerts. Audiences paid in advance for a whole series of concerts and these made money. The family could afford a large flat, with six big rooms, a kitchen, loft and cellar.

Perhaps the highlight of Leopold's visit before he went home was when Haydn told him, 'your son is the greatest composer known to me'.

Mozart had written an opera in German, '*Il Seraglio*' in 1782. In 1786 he enthusiastically composed 'The Marriage of Figaro', in Italian, a daring story of a rebellious servant. The words were by Da Ponte, an Italian poet and teacher who later worked in London and New

This unfinished portrait of Mozart was painted by his brother in law in 1789.

York. Figaro's tunes were whistled everywhere, played by harpists in bars and arranged for dances and for the piano, as well as wind quintets.

An English singer, Nancy Storace, who sang in the very first performance of the opera, invited Mozart to England. He longed to go, but Leopold, who was already looking after Nannerl's child, didn't want to look after little Karl and the new baby Johann as well.

Although he was working furiously, Mozart still found time to fit in pupils he thought promising. He took on an Englishman called Thomas Attwood, and wrote jokingly on his music, 'You are an ass'. Beethoven at sixteen travelled miles to have lessons from Wolfgang. He couldn't stay on because his mother was ill, but Mozart heard him play and said, 'Watch out for him. He will make a stir all over the world.'

Mozart's next masterpiece, *Don Giovanni* was written to be performed at the wedding celebrations of the Emperor's niece. In fact it had its first performance in Prague where it had a marvellous reception. It was then shown in Vienna. His next opera, *Cosi Fan Tutte* didn't have such a good reception. Constanze said that she didn't like the story, which was about unfaithful lovers, although she knew that the music would make up for it.

Early in 1787, Leopold became ill, and in May, he died. Mozart wrote to his sister that he couldn't leave Vienna, where he was as busy as ever. Mozart had relied on Leopold all his life. For years they had sent each other letters full of their shared passion for music. In spite of his sadness, Mozart composed *Eine Kleine Nachtmusik*, (*A Little Night Music*), which became one of his most popular works.

Of the many flats in which Mozart and Constanze lived, this was the best. It was here that Leopold met Haydn.

The following year, war broke out between Austria and Turkey. Mozart found that people didn't want to go to concerts so much. Yet in 1788 he composed three magnificent symphonies: no 39, the well-known no. 40 and the 41st, nicknamed the 'Jupiter'. Although he was composing at an astonishing rate, he began to fall into debt. He had never been a good manager, and he and Constanze often spent more money than they had.

Constanze's health was poor and she had to go for expensive treatments at Baden, near Vienna. After six pregnancies, she was often unwell. Of her four sons and two daughters only Karl and Wolfgang survived. When she was ill at home, Mozart used to tiptoe round with his finger to his lips. He sat by her bed, composing, and when he cut himself badly with his penknife when he was sharpening a quill pen, he didn't make any fuss in case he disturbed her.

To relax, Mozart played billiards and loved dancing. A friend said that he once found Mozart and Constanze dancing together to keep warm when they didn't have enough money for firewood.

In 1789, Mozart went on a tour round Germany, but he was still borrowing money wherever he could. He had a job, as Chamber Musician at the Emperor's court, but it wasn't well paid and most of the work was composing dances for balls. The following year he composed very little.

Then more opportunities came up, including the chance to work on an opera in England, but Mozart could not leave his young family. An actor friend called Schikaneder asked him to write a fantasy opera, *The Magic Flute* for his theatre company.

A scene from The Magic Flute

Mozart was lonely when Constanze was away, although he wrote her many loving and teasing letters. He received a mysterious request from an anonymous benefactor for a Requiem or mass for the dead. Exhausted by overwork, he began to believe that he was writing his own requiem. He became so ill, he thought he might have been poisoned by a jealous rival.

The Magic Flute was a triumph. Mozart lay in bed with his watch on his pillow, imagining the performances. He asked Constanze and their friends to help him sing through part of the unfinished requiem. He was offered a new job at St Stephen's cathedral, which would have given him more money and the freedom to compose as he longed to do. But it was too late.

Mozart died on 5th December 1791. He was thirty-five years old. Constanze was left with a four month old baby and a young child. She was near to collapse. Mozart was given the cheapest possible funeral, blessed at St Stephen's cathedral, and taken to an unmarked grave in Saint Marx cemetery.

After Mozart died, Constanze helped to write his biography.

Mozart's sons, Karl and Wolfgang.

His two sons were both talented, but only young Wolfgang made music his career. Neither of them married, so there were no more Mozarts. Constanze worked hard to have her husband's work performed and published after his death and helped her second husband to prepare Mozart's biography. She moved back to Salzburg where she lived near Nannerl, but they were never close friends.

Mozart's story does not end with his death. In 1795 Constanze organised a benefit concert of Mozart's last opera. Beethoven played one of Mozart's piano concertos between the acts. Since then composers, performers and listeners have been inspired by Mozart's music, which is still enjoyed all over the world.

Index